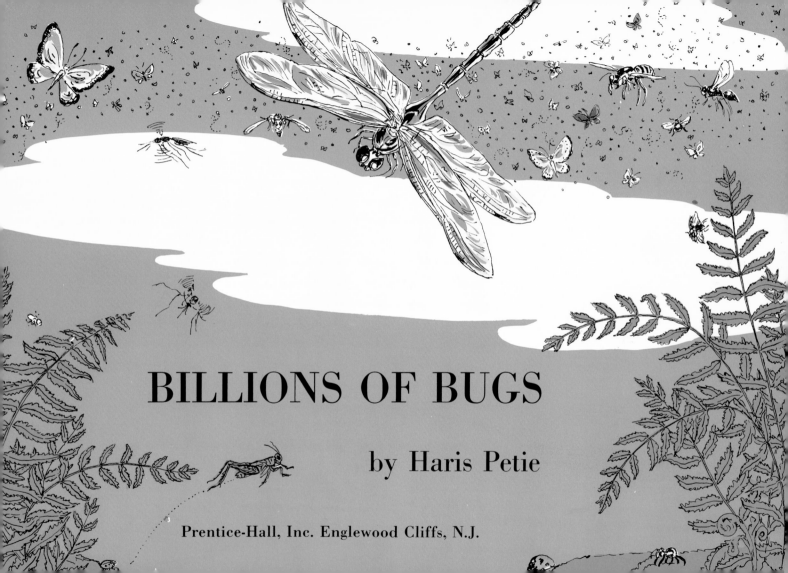

BILLIONS OF BUGS

by Haris Petie

Prentice-Hall, Inc. Englewood Cliffs, N.J.

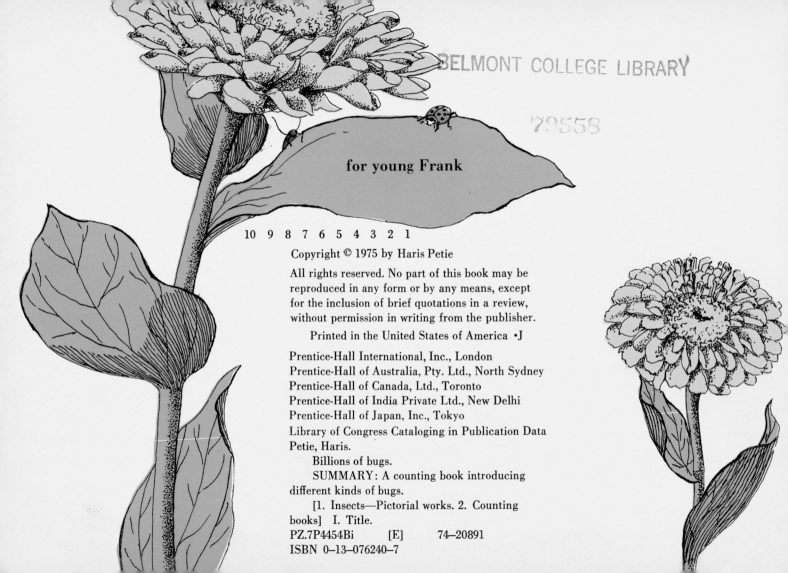

for young Frank

10 9 8 7 6 5 4 3 2 1

Copyright © 1975 by Haris Petie

Printed in the United States of America •J

Prentice-Hall International, Inc., London
Prentice-Hall of Australia, Pty. Ltd., North Sydney
Prentice-Hall of Canada, Ltd., Toronto
Prentice-Hall of India Private Ltd., New Delhi
Prentice-Hall of Japan, Inc., Tokyo
Library of Congress Cataloging in Publication Data
Petie, Haris.
      Billions of bugs.
      SUMMARY: A counting book introducing
different kinds of bugs.
      [1. Insects—Pictorial works. 2. Counting
books]   I. Title.
PZ.7P4454Bi   [E]   74–20891
ISBN 0–13–076240–7

1 Praying mantis eating a grub

10 Walking sticks hide in a shrub

20 Dragonflies buzz in the sky

30 Grasshoppers jumping by

40 Earwigs are hard to see

50 Inchworms move silently

60 Mosquitoes ready to bite

70 Baby spiders come into sight

80 Vine chafers sitting very still

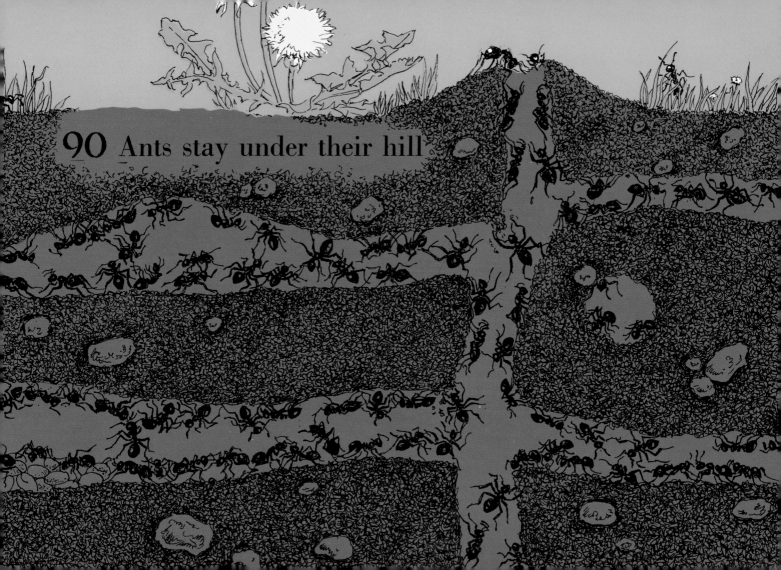

90 Ants stay under their hill

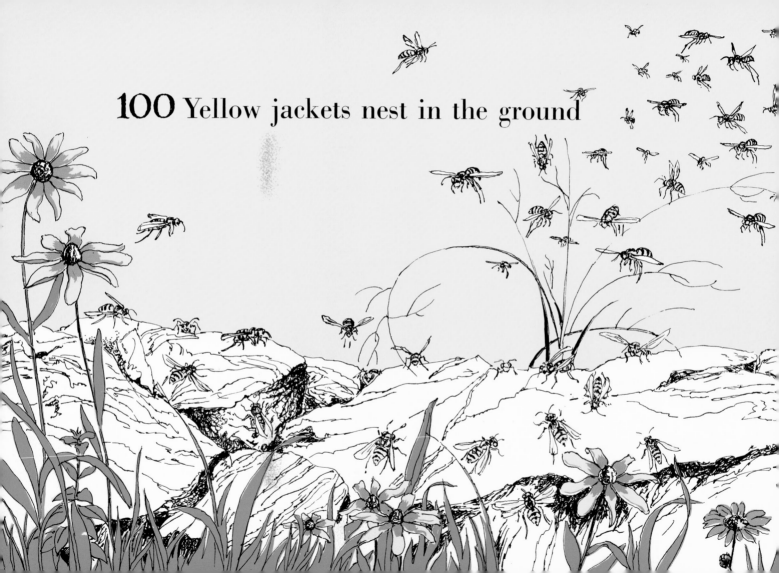

100 Yellow jackets nest in the ground

200
Fireflies flash all around.

300 Fleas leap across the floor

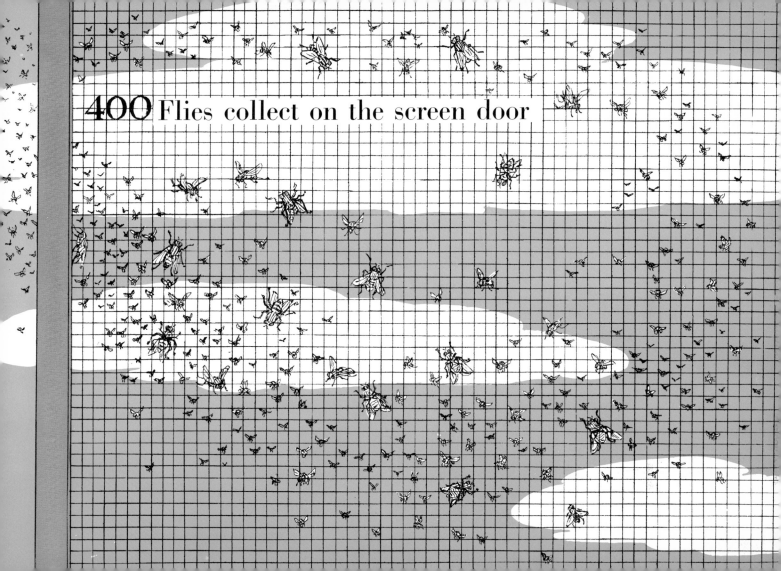

400 Flies collect on the screen door

500 Hornets fly to their home

600
Bees make honey in their combs

700 Lady bugs fly about
or repose

800 Aphids suck on a rose

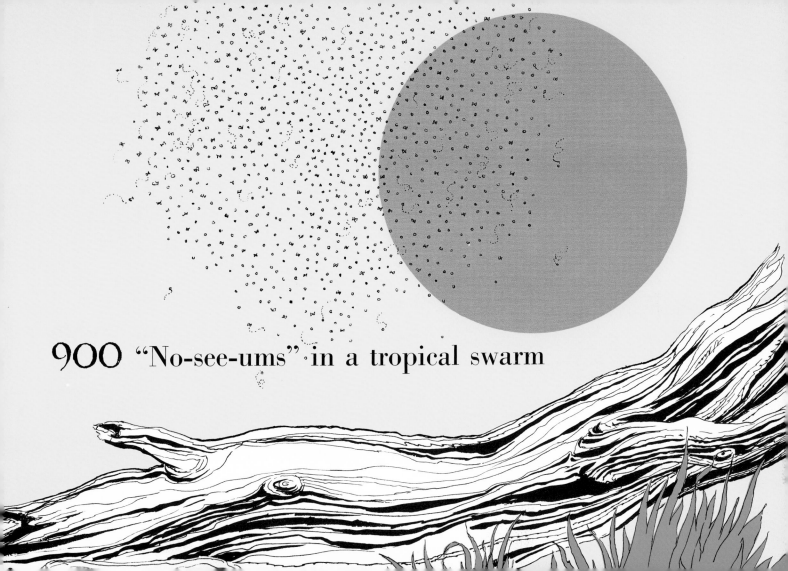

900 "No-see-ums" in a tropical swarm

1000 Butterflies fly south
where it's warm

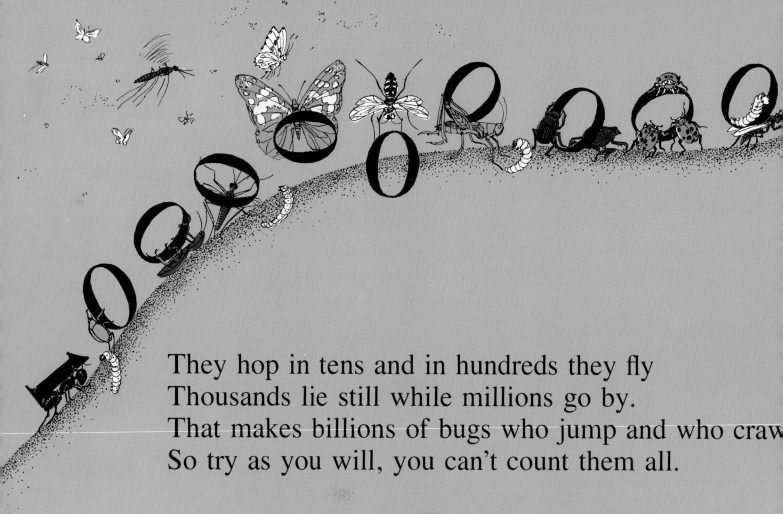

They hop in tens and in hundreds they fly
Thousands lie still while millions go by.
That makes billions of bugs who jump and who craw
So try as you will, you can't count them all.